I Like Biographies!

Read About
Harriet Tubman

Stephen Feinstein

Enslow Elementary
an imprint of
Enslow Publishers, Inc.

40 Industrial Road   PO Box 38
Box 398   Aldershot
Berkeley Heights, NJ 07922 Hants GU12 6BP
USA   UK

http://www.enslow.com

Words to Know

conductor—On the Underground Railroad, a person who helped other slaves escape.

overseer—A person who was in charge of the slaves working in the fields.

plantation—A large farm in the South.

slave—A person who works for someone else against their will.

Underground Railroad—A secret group of homes where escaping slaves could stay on their way North.

Enslow Elementary, an imprint of Enslow Publishers, Inc.

Enslow Elementary® is a registered trademark of Enslow Publishers, Inc.

Copyright © 2005 by Enslow Publishers, Inc.

All rights reserved.

No part of this book may be reproduced by any means without the written permission of the publisher.

Library of Congress Cataloging-in-Publication Data

Feinstein, Stephen.
    Read about Harriet Tubman / Stephen Feinstein.
        p. cm. — (I like biographies!)
    Includes bibliographical references and index.
    ISBN 0-7660-2591-8
    1. Tubman, Harriet, 1820?–1913—Juvenile literature. 2. Slaves—United States—Biography—Juvenile literature. 3. African American women—Biography—Juvenile literature. 4. African Americans—Biography—Juvenile literature. 5. Underground railroad—Juvenile literature. I. Title. II. Series.
    E444.T82F45 2005
    973.7'115'092—dc22
            [B]
                2004010623

Printed in the United States of America

10 9 8 7 6 5 4 3 2 1

To Our Readers: We have done our best to make sure all Internet Addresses in this book were active and appropriate when we went to press. However, the author and the publisher have no control over and assume no liability for the material available on those Internet sites or on links to other Web sites. Any comments or suggestions can be sent by e-mail to comments@enslow.com or to the address on the back cover.

Every effort has been made to locate all copyright holders of material used in this book. If any errors or omissions have occurred, corrections will be made in future editions.

Illustration Credits: AP/Wide World, p.19; Library of Congress, pp. 1, 5, 11, 21; North Wind Picture Archives, pp. 3, 7, 9, 13, 15; Photographs and Prints Division, Schomburg Center for Research in Black Culture, The New York Public Library, Astor, Lenox and Tilden Foundations, p. 17.

Cover Illustration: Photo by Peter Gamble, courtesy of www.BlackCommentator.com.

Contents

1 Growing Up on a Plantation 4

2 Harriet Dreams of Freedom 10

3 The Underground Railroad 14

4 Harriet Becomes a Conductor. . . 18

Timeline 22

Learn More 23

Index 24

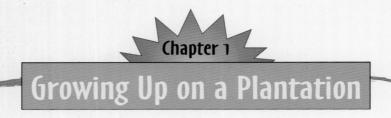

Chapter 1

Growing Up on a Plantation

Harriet Tubman was born about 1820 on a plantation in Maryland. Her parents, Harriet and Benjamin Ross, were slaves. They and their eleven children belonged to the owner of the plantation.

This picture of a slave family was taken in 1862. Slaves worked hard and had no freedom.

There were many slaves on the plantation. They worked hard in the fields from morning to night. They were not paid for their work. The overseer beat them with a whip if they did not work fast enough.

These slave children are picking sugar cane and carrying water. The overseer is the man in the white hat.

When Harriet was six years old, she was sent off to work at a nearby plantation. One day she ran away. She hid for a few days in the pigpen. When she went back to the house, she was sick. She could not do much work. Harriet was soon sent back to her old plantation. Now she had to work in the fields picking cotton and corn.

These slaves are picking cotton, like Harriet did. It was hard work.

As the years went by, Harriet became very strong from her hard work. She liked working outside. But she hated being a slave. Two of Harriet's sisters were sold to another plantation. Harriet was afraid that one day she would be sold and would never see her family again.

In this picture, a man is being sold away from his family. Harriet was afraid that this would happen to her, too.

THE PARTING "Buy us too."

In 1844, Harriet married John Tubman. He had been a slave, but was now free. Harriet also wanted to be free. She began to dream of escaping to the North. In the North, black people lived in freedom. But John did not share her dreams. So Harriet made up her mind to run away by herself.

Like the woman in this picture, Harriet hated being a slave. She dreamed of running away and being free.

13

Chapter 3

The Underground Railroad

In 1849, Harriet found out that she was going to be sold to a plantation far away. The time had come for her to make a break for freedom.

Harriet knew that some white people who were against slavery helped runaway slaves escape. The secret way to the North was called the Underground Railroad. Friendly homes were called stations.

The Underground Railroad was not really a railroad. It was a group of homes where slaves could stay on their way North. These escaped slaves are going through a swamp.

15

One night Harriet slipped away from the plantation. She walked all night through the woods. She stopped at her first station in Bucktown, Maryland.

Every night she walked many miles through woods and swamps. During the day she hid in Underground Railroad stations. Harriet finally reached Pennsylvania, a free state.

In this picture, Harriet is standing at the left. This photograph was probably taken many years after the Civil War. This means that the people in it are free, not slaves.

In Pennsylvania, Harriet found jobs cooking and cleaning. Over the next few years, she made nineteen trips back to Maryland. She became a conductor on the Underground Railroad.

It was against the law to help a runaway slave. But this did not stop Harriet. She led about three hundred slaves, including her family, to freedom in the North.

Harriet was never caught, and she never lost a slave. This statue in Massachusetts honors her and the other slaves who escaped.

During the Civil War, which lasted from 1861 to 1865, Harriet was a nurse and a spy for the Union Army. In 1865, the United States passed a law making all slaves free. After the war, Harriet lived in Auburn, New York.

Harriet Tubman died on March 10, 1913. She was over ninety years old. Her brave work for freedom will never be forgotten.

Harriet spent the rest of her life helping sick, poor, and older black people. Even when she was very old herself, she still kept helping.

Timeline

About 1820—Harriet is born on a plantation in Maryland.

1844—Harriet marries John Tubman.

1849—Harriet runs away from the plantation to Pennsylvania.

1850—Harriet becomes a conductor on the Underground Railroad, helping slaves to escape.

1861–1865—Harriet works as a nurse, spy, and scout during the Civil War.

1908—Harriet builds a home for poor and old black people in Auburn, New York.

1913—Harriet Tubman dies on March 10.

Learn More

Books

Gayle, Sharon. *Harriet Tubman and the Freedom Train.* New York: Aladdin Paperbacks, 2003.

Kulling, Monica. *Escape North! The Story of Harriet Tubman.* New York: Random House, 2000.

Lawrence, Jacob. *Harriet and the Promised Land.* New York: Simon & Schuster, 1993.

Rappaport, Doreen. *Freedom River.* New York: Hyperion Books for Children, 2000.

Internet Addresses

New York History Net: The Harriet Tubman Home
    <http://www.nyhistory.com/harriettubman/>

The Underground Railroad
    <http://www.nationalgeographic.com/features/99/railroad/j2.html>

Index

Auburn, New York, 20

Civil War, 20

Maryland, 4, 16, 18

overseer, 6

Pennsylvania, 16, 18
plantation, 4, 6, 8, 10,
    14, 16

Ross, Harriet, 4
Ross, John, 4

stations, 14, 16

Tubman, Harriet
    as a conductor, 18
    as a nurse, 20
    as a spy, 20
    childhood, 4, 8, 10
    death, 20
    escape from slavery,
        14, 16
Tubman, John, 12

Underground Railroad,
    14, 16, 18
Union Army, 20

Tao Te Ching

Tao Te Ching

Lao Tzu

Translated by
John H. McDonald

Introduction by
John Baldock

This edition published in 2018 by Arcturus Publishing Limited
26/27 Bickels Yard, 151–153 Bermondsey Street,
London SE1 3HA

Copyright © Arcturus Holdings Limited

AD006314UK

Printed in the UK

CONTENTS

Introduction 7

Tao Te Ching............. 19

INTRODUCTION

The *Tao Te Ching* is not only the most influential classic text of Chinese philosophy, it is also one of the most widely read examples of what can perhaps best be described as 'wisdom literature'.

According to tradition, the *Tao Te Ching* was written in the 6th century BC by the Taoist sage Lao Tzu, a contemporary of Confucius (K'ung Fu-tzu, 551–479BC). However, analysis of the text's vocabulary and style suggests a date some time in the late 4th or early 3rd century BC. Several ancient versions of the Chinese text exist, but the oldest extant version was discovered in 1993 in a tomb near the town of Guodian in Hubei Province. Written on numerous slips of bamboo, a common writing material in ancient China, this text has been dated prior to 300BC. Initially the text was known simply as the Lao Tzu, but during the Han period (1st century BC to 1st century AD) it became more widely known under its present name of the *Tao Te Ching* – a title that derives from the traditional division of the book's 81 short chapters into two sections. The first section (Chapters 1 to 37) opens

with an explanation of the enigmatic nature of the Tao (literally, 'the Way'), while the second (Chapters 38 to 81) opens with an explanation of the workings of *Te* (virtue, power, quality or 'the good'). The third word, namely *Ching*, means 'classic', and so *Tao Te Ching* can be translated as 'The Classic Book of the Way and its Power (or Virtue)'.

Although the *Tao Te Ching* is of primary importance for the Taoist school of Chinese philosophy as well as the Taoist religion and Chinese Buddhism, its translation into hundreds of languages has made it available to a worldwide audience. The original text comprised around 5,000 Chinese characters, some of which have multiple meanings; it was also written in a cryptic style. If we add to this the differences between Chinese and Western thought and the passage of time between the writing of the original text and the present day, we can begin to appreciate the difficulties faced by translators in their efforts to provide an effective translation of the *Tao Te Ching* that is accessible to a modern Western audience. In spite of these difficulties, over forty translations exist in print in English alone, plus thirty or more online. However, a simple, side-by-side comparison of two or more translations will reveal the wide-ranging differences in interpretation adopted by individual translators, but

this is hardly surprising in view of the enigmatic nature of the Tao itself and the ambiguous style of the *Tao Te Ching*.

John H. McDonald, the author of the translation presented here, consulted a number of different versions of the text in an attempt to find a consensus between them and produce a definitive translation of this ancient Chinese classic.

Most translations refer to the Sage or Master as being exclusively masculine in gender, but McDonald chose the feminine because 'a Master is aware of both, but chooses the least likely of the two', as the following verse shows:

Know the masculine,
but keep to the feminine:
and become a watershed to the world.
(Chapter 28)

LAO TZU

The little we know about Lao Tzu comes from the *Shi chi* (Records of the Historian) compiled towards the beginning of the 1st century BC by the Han historian Ssu-ma Ch'ien (145–85BC).

The name 'Lao Tzu' is actually an honorific title

meaning 'Old Master' – according to Ssu-ma Ch'ien, his given name was Li Er Tan. Born in the village of Chu Jen in the state of Ch'u, he became an archivist at the court of the Chou Dynasty in later life. Ssu-ma Ch'ien also recounts two events from Lao Tzu's life.

The first of these was a visit by Confucius, who asked Lao Tzu to tutor him in the traditional rites. Lao Tzu replied in words that express some of the central themes of the *Tao Te Ching*, saying, 'Those you talk about have turned to dust. All that remains is their words. When a nobleman lives in good times, he goes to court in a carriage. But when times are hard, he goes where the wind blows. Some people say that a wise merchant hides his wealth and thus appears to be poor. Likewise the sage: if he has great inner virtue, he appears outwardly to be a fool. Stop being so arrogant with all your questions, your self-importance and your overbearing obsessions. None of this is the real you. That is all I have to say to you.'

When Confucius rejoined his followers, he described his meeting with Lao Tzu thus: 'I know that birds fly, fish swim and animals run. Creatures that run can be trapped; those that swim can be caught in nets; those that fly can be shot down. But what to do with a dragon, I do not know. It rides on the clouds and the wind. Today I met

Lao Tzu, and he is like a dragon.'

The second event related by Ssu-ma Ch'ien is the final journey of Lao Tzu. Despairing at the moral decline of the kingdom and people's obsessive desire for possessions and status, Lao Tzu set off on a water buffalo to travel to the West. (According to some traditions he was withdrawing from the world to become a hermit, but the story takes on a slightly different meaning when we consider that in Chinese mythology 'the West' is the land of the afterlife.) When he reached the western gate of the kingdom in the mountain pass at Hang-ku, he was recognized as a sage by Kuan Yin, the Keeper of the Pass, who asked Lao Tzu to write down his knowledge of the Tao before retiring from the world. Lao Tzu duly obliged and, according to tradition, wrote the book in one night. The next day the sage presented the book to Kuan Yin, saying, 'This book is no different from other books in that it is a dead thing, but you can bring it to life if you put into practice what is written in it.' With that, Lao Tzu mounted his water buffalo and departed for the West, never to be seen again.

Whether or not a single individual known as Lao Tzu, the 'Old Master', was the author of the *Tao Te Ching* is now openly questioned by many scholars, as is his historical existence. Instead, it is suggested that the text

is more in the nature of an anthology of sayings compiled over an extended period of time before taking its present form. What is beyond question, however, is the profound nature of the universal wisdom contained in this seminal work on the Tao.

The *Tao Te Ching*

The *Tao Te Ching* is essentially about the Tao, but a number of related themes recur throughout the text.

The most significant of these are the Sage or Master, rulers and government, and non-action (*wu-wei*).

The *Tao*

The Chinese word *Tao* is generally translated as 'the Way', the implication being that it refers to a spiritual way or path. It also has a much wider, more enigmatic meaning than this, as indicated by the opening lines of the *Tao Te Ching*:

> *The tao that can be described*
> *is not the eternal Tao.*
> *The name that can be spoken*
> *is not the eternal Name. (1)*

The *Tao Te Ching* goes on to tell us that the Tao is not only 'older than the concept of God' (4), it is both 'intangible and evasive' (21) and therefore beyond all concepts. It 'may be regarded as the Mother of the universe' (25) for 'it alone nourishes and completes all things' (41). The Tao 'has always existed' and is even 'beyond existing and not existing' (21), from which we can infer that the Tao denotes an ultimate 'way', the Way of Absolute Reality (i.e. reality purely and simply 'as it is', unadulterated by our concepts and opinions). Yet when the Tao is 'looked at, there is nothing for [people] to see. When listened for, there is nothing for them to hear' (35). Moreover, 'the world cannot understand it' (62) since the Tao lies beyond the grasp of our normal understanding. Or, as the *Tao Te Ching* tells us elsewhere, 'our basic understandings are not from the Tao because they come from the depths of our misunderstanding' (38).

If we wish to increase our capacity for understanding and thereby draw closer to the Tao, we are advised to change our way of thinking because 'the more knowledge you seek, the less you will understand' (47). We are encouraged to follow the example of the Master who 'learns by unlearning, thus she is able to understand all things' (64).

THE SAGE OR MASTER

The Sage or Master is one who, having become 'unlearned' by emptying him- or herself of all concepts and opinions, is 'filled with the Tao [and] is like a newborn child' (55). Having 'attained unity with the Tao' (39), the Master no longer has a 'self' (13). That is to say, he or she has attained a state of consciousness which is very different from the state we normally experience because 'the Master has no mind of her own' (49). His or her consciousness is as one with the Tao which is itself 'without wants and desires' (34), and so the Master is no longer governed by the whims and desires of the ego: 'freed from desire, you can see the hidden mystery. By having desire, you can only see what is visibly real' (1). As the Master freely admits, 'I am different from ordinary people. I nurse from the Great Mother's [Tao's] breasts' (20).

> Once we have found the Mother,
> we begin to know what Her children should be.
> When we know we are the Mother's child,
> we begin to guard the qualities of the Mother in us. (52)

Because the Master is filled with the qualities or virtues

of the Tao, we find the *Tao Te Ching* employing similar expressions for both – for example, the Tao is likened to 'the Uncarved Block' (28), while the Master, whose union with the Tao has brought about his or her completion, is 'whole as an uncarved block of wood' (15); the Tao 'never acts with force' (37), likewise the Master 'shuns the use of violence' (60); the Tao 'does not compete' (73) and 'the Tao of the Wise Person acts by not competing' (81).

RULERS AND GOVERNMENT

The historian Ssu-ma Ch'ien relates Lao Tzu's departure for the West during a period of moral decline. As we have seen, however, Ssu-ma Ch'ien's traditional 6th-century BC dating for the writing of the *Tao Te Ching* differs from the scholastic view that places it much later, in the late 4th or early 3rd century BC, during the aptly named Warring States Period (480–222BC) – a period when regional warlords sought to annex smaller states in the declining years of the Chou dynasty. Significantly, both datings point to the *Tao Te Ching* having been written during a time of moral and political decline – a fitting context for the guidance it offers to those who rule or govern.

According to the *Tao Te Ching*, 'the best leaders are

those the people hardly know exist' (17); they 'become servants of their people' (68) for 'only he who is the lowest servant of the kingdom, is worthy of becoming its ruler' (78). Good government 'is unobtrusive' and thus enables the people to 'become whole' (58). It doesn't interfere with the people unnecessarily:

> *Governing a large country*
> *is like frying small fish.*
> *Too much poking spoils the meat. (60)*

Wise rulers are those who 'follow the way of the Tao' (37), for 'if a ruler abides by its principles, then her people will willingly follow' (32).

NON-ACTION OR WU-WEI

The *Tao Te Ching* tells us that 'true sayings seem contradictory' (78), and there are possibly few sayings more contradictory than those relating to the principle of non-action or *wu-wei*. For example, we are advised to

> *Act by not acting;*
> *do by not doing. (63)*

And we are told that

The Master... accomplishes much without
doing anything. (47)

In mastering the ego or 'self' rather than allowing it to master him/her, the Master is freed from the need to act out of personal desire or self-interest and thus becomes an empty vehicle for the Tao. In this liberated state of 'being' rather than 'doing', the Master enjoys that ultimate freedom – the 'freedom of no-choice' – because he/she does nothing; it is the Tao which accomplishes things through the Master.

For those who practise not-doing,
everything will fall into place. (3)

The *Tao Te Ching* was written 2,500 years ago. In many respects the world is now a very different place, thanks to advances in science and technology, transport and communication, and the emergence of the global economy. Yet in others the world is much the same as it was in the Warring States Period, for we are still fighting wars, still thirsting after power and status and still obsessed with

the acquisition of wealth and possessions. In that respect, the timeless wisdom that lies at the heart of the *Tao Te Ching* is just as relevant today as it was 2,500 years ago.

> *Embrace simplicity.*
> *Put others first.*
> *Desire little. (19)*

> *Without opening your door,*
> *you can know the whole world.*
> *Without looking out of your window,*
> *you can understand the way of the Tao. (47)*

John Baldock

TAO TE CHING

1

The tao that can be described
is not the eternal Tao.
The name that can be spoken
is not the eternal Name.

The nameless is the boundary of Heaven
    and Earth.
The named is the mother of creation.

Freed from desire, you can see the hidden
    mystery.
By having desire, you can only see what is
    visibly real.

Yet mystery and reality
emerge from the same source.
This source is called darkness.

Darkness born from darkness.
The beginning of all understanding.

2

When people see things as beautiful,
ugliness is created.
When people see things as good,
evil is created.

Being and non-being produce each other.
Difficult and easy complement each other.
Long and short define each other.
High and low oppose each other.
Fore and aft follow each other.
Therefore the Master
can act without doing anything
and teach without saying a word.
Things come her way and she does not
    stop them;
things leave and she lets them go.
She has without possessing,
and acts without any expectations.
When her work is done, she takes no credit.
That is why it will last forever.

3

If you overesteem talented individuals,
people will become overly competitive.
If you overvalue possessions,
people will begin to steal.

Do not display your treasures
or people will become envious.

The Master leads by
emptying people's minds,
filling their bellies,
weakening their ambitions,
and making them become strong.
Preferring simplicity and freedom
      from desires,
avoiding the pitfalls of knowledge and
      wrong action.

For those who practise not-doing,
everything will fall into place.

4

The Tao is like an empty container:
it can never be emptied and can
     never be filled.
Infinitely deep, it is the source of all things.
It dulls the sharp, unties the knotted,
     shades the lighted, and unites all of
     creation with dust.

It is hidden but always present.
I don't know who gave birth to it.
It is older than the concept of God.

5

Heaven and Earth are impartial;
they treat all of creation as straw dogs.
The Master doesn't take sides;
she treats everyone like a straw dog.

The space between Heaven and Earth is
    like a bellows;
it is empty, yet has not lost its power.
The more it is used, the more it produces;
the more you talk of it, the less you
    comprehend.

It is better not to speak of things you do
    not understand.

6

The spirit of emptiness is immortal.
It is called the Great Mother
because it gives birth to Heaven and Earth.

It is like a vapour,
barely seen but always present.
Use it effortlessly.

7

The Tao of Heaven is eternal,
and the earth is long enduring.
Why are they long enduring?
They do not live for themselves;
thus they are present for all beings.

The Master puts herself last;
and finds herself in the place of authority.
She detaches herself from all things;
therefore she is united with all things.
She gives no thought to self.
She is perfectly fulfilled.

8

The supreme good is like water,
which benefits all of creation
without trying to compete with it.
It gathers in unpopular places.
Thus it is like the Tao.

The location makes the dwelling good.
Depth of understanding makes the mind
    good.
A kind heart makes the giving good.
Integrity makes the government good.
Accomplishment makes your labours good.
Proper timing makes a decision good.

Only when there is no competition
will we all live in peace.

9

It is easier to carry an empty cup
than one that is filled to the brim.

The sharper the knife,
the easier it is to dull.
The more wealth you possess,
the harder it is to protect.
Pride brings its own trouble.

When you have accomplished your goal,
simply walk away.
This is the pathway to Heaven.

10

Nurture the darkness of your soul
until you become whole.
Can you do this and not fail?
Can you focus your life-breath until you
     become
supple as a newborn child?
While you cleanse your inner vision
will you be found without fault?
Can you love people and lead them
without forcing your will on them?
When Heaven gives and takes away,
can you be content with the outcome?
When you understand all things,
can you step back from your own
     understanding?

Giving birth and nourishing,
making without possessing,
expecting nothing in return.
To grow, yet not to control:
This is the mysterious virtue.

11

Thirty spokes are joined together in a
    wheel,
but it is the centre hole
that allows the wheel to function.

We mould clay into a pot,
but it is the emptiness inside
that makes the vessel useful.

We fashion wood for a house,
but it is the emptiness inside
that makes it liveable.

We work with the substantial,
but the emptiness is what we use.

12

Five colours blind the eye.
Five notes deafen the ear.
Five flavours make the palate go stale.
Too much activity deranges the mind.
Too much wealth causes crime.
The Master acts on what she feels and not
    what she sees.
She shuns the latter, and prefers to seek the
    former.

13

Success is as dangerous as failure,
and we are often our own worst enemy.

What does it mean that success is as dangerous
as failure?
He who is superior is also someone's subordinate.
Receiving favour and losing it both cause alarm.
That is what is meant by success is as dangerous
as failure.
What does it mean that we are often our own
worst enemy?
The reason I have an enemy is because I have 'self'.
If I no longer had a 'self', I would no longer have
an enemy.

Love the whole world as if it were your self;
then you will truly care for all things.

14

Look for it, and it can't be seen.
Listen for it, and it can't be heard.
Grasp for it, and it can't be caught.
These three cannot be further described,
so we treat them as The One.

Its highest is not bright.
Its depths are not dark.
Unending, unnameable, it returns to nothingness.
Formless forms, and imageless images,
subtle, beyond all understanding.

Approach it and you will not see a beginning;
follow it and there will be no end.
When we grasp the Tao of the ancient ones,
we can use it to direct our life today.
To know the ancient origin of Tao:
this is the beginning of wisdom.

15

The Sages of old were profound
and knew the ways of subtlety and discernment.
Their wisdom is beyond our comprehension.
Because their knowledge was so far superior
I can only give a poor description.

They were careful
as someone crossing a frozen stream in winter.
Alert as if surrounded on all sides by the enemy.
Courteous as a guest.
Fluid as melting ice.
Whole as an uncarved block of wood.
Receptive as a valley.
Turbid as muddied water.

Who can be still
until their mud settles
and the water is cleared by itself?
Can you remain tranquil until right action occurs
        by itself?

The Master doesn't seek fulfilment.
For only those who are not full are able to be used,
which brings the feeling of completeness.

16

If you can empty your mind of all thoughts
your heart will embrace the tranquillity of peace.
Watch the workings of all of creation,
but contemplate their return to the source.

All creatures in the universe
return to the point where they began.
Returning to the source is tranquillity
because we submit to Heaven's mandate.

Returning to Heaven's mandate is called being
    constant.
Knowing the constant is called 'enlightenment'.
Not knowing the constant is the source of evil deeds
because we have no roots.
By knowing the constant we can accept things as
    they are.
By accepting things as they are, we become impartial.
By being impartial, we become one with Heaven.
By being one with Heaven, we become one with Tao.
Being one with Tao, we are no longer concerned
    about losing our life because we know the Tao is
    constant and we are one with Tao.

17

The best leaders are those the people hardly
        know exist.
The next best is a leader who is loved and praised.
Next comes the one who is feared.
The worst one is the leader who is despised.

If you don't trust the people,
they will become untrustworthy.

The best leaders value their words, and use them
        sparingly.
When the Master has accomplished her task,
the people say, 'Amazing:
we did it, all by ourselves!'

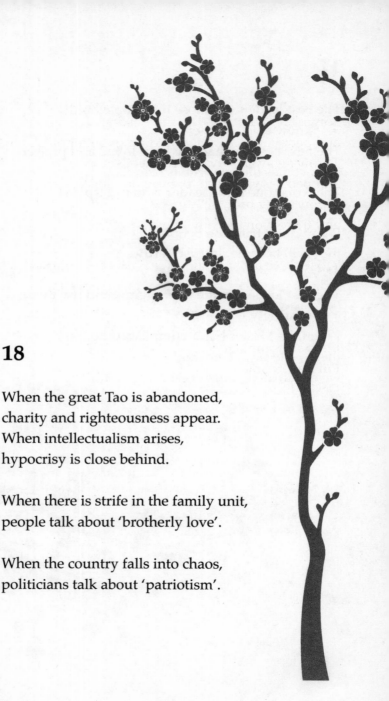

18

When the great Tao is abandoned,
charity and righteousness appear.
When intellectualism arises,
hypocrisy is close behind.

When there is strife in the family unit,
people talk about 'brotherly love'.

When the country falls into chaos,
politicians talk about 'patriotism'.

19

Forget about knowledge and wisdom,
and people will be a hundred times better off.
Throw away charity and righteousness,
and people will return to brotherly love.
Throw away profit and greed,
and there won't be any thieves.

These three are superficial and aren't enough
to keep us at the centre of the circle, so we must
      also:

Embrace simplicity.
Put others first.
Desire little.

20

Renounce knowledge and your problems will end.
What is the difference between yes and no?
What is the difference between good and evil?
Must you fear what others fear?
Nonsense, look how far you have missed the
    mark!

Other people are joyous,
as though they were at a spring festival.
I alone am unconcerned and expressionless,
like an infant before it has learned to smile.
Other people have more than they need;
I alone seem to possess nothing.
I am lost and drift about with no place to go.
I am like a fool, my mind is in chaos.

Ordinary people are bright;
I alone am dark.
Ordinary people are clever;
I alone am dull.
Ordinary people seem discriminating;
I alone am muddled and confused.
I drift on the waves on the ocean,
blown at the mercy of the wind.
Other people have their goals,
I alone am dull and uncouth.

I am different from ordinary people.
I nurse from the Great Mother's breasts.

21

The greatest virtue you can have
comes from following only the Tao;
which takes a form that is intangible and evasive.

Even though the Tao is intangible and evasive,
we are able to know it exists.
Intangible and evasive, yet it has a manifestation.
Secluded and dark, yet there is a vitality within it.
Its vitality is very genuine.
Within it we can find order.

Since the beginning of time, the Tao has always
    existed.
It is beyond existing and not existing.
How do I know where creation comes from?
I look inside myself and see it.

22

If you want to become whole,
first let yourself become broken.
If you want to become straight,
first let yourself become twisted.
If you want to become full,
first let yourself become empty.
If you want to become new,
first let yourself become old.
Those whose desires are few get them,
those whose desires are great go astray.

For this reason the Master embraces the Tao,
as an example for the world to follow.
Because she isn't self-centred,
people can see the light in her.
Because she does not boast of herself,
she becomes a shining example.
Because she does not glorify herself,
she becomes a person of merit.
Because she wants nothing from the world,
the world cannot overcome her.
When the ancient Masters said,
'If you want to become whole,
then first let yourself be broken,'
they weren't using empty words.
All who do this will be made complete.

23

Nature uses few words:
when the gale blows, it will not last long;
when it rains hard, it lasts but a little while;
What causes these to happen? Heaven and Earth.

Why do we humans go on endlessly about little
when nature does much in a little time?
If you open yourself to the Tao,
you and Tao become one.
If you open yourself to Virtue,
then you can become virtuous.
If you open yourself to loss,
then you will become lost.

If you open yourself to the Tao,
the Tao will eagerly welcome you.
If you open yourself to virtue,
virtue will become a part of you.
If you open yourself to loss,
the lost are glad to see you.

When you do not trust people,
people will become untrustworthy.

24

Those who stand on tiptoes
do not stand firmly.
Those who rush ahead
don't get very far.
Those who try to outshine others
dim their own light.
Those who call themselves righteous
can't know how wrong they are.
Those who boast of their accomplishments
diminish the things they have done.

Compared to the Tao, these actions are unworthy.
If we are to follow the Tao, we must not do
    these things.

25

Before the universe was born
there was something in the chaos of the heavens.
It stands alone and empty,
solitary and unchanging.
It is ever present and secure.
It may be regarded as the Mother of the universe.
Because I do not know its name,
I call it the Tao.
If forced to give it a name,
I would call it 'Great'.

Because it is Great means it is everywhere.
Being everywhere means it is eternal.
Being eternal means everything returns to it.

Tao is great.
Heaven is great.
Earth is great.
Humanity is great.
Within the universe, these are the four great things.

Humanity follows the earth.
Earth follows Heaven.
Heaven follows the Tao.
The Tao follows only itself.

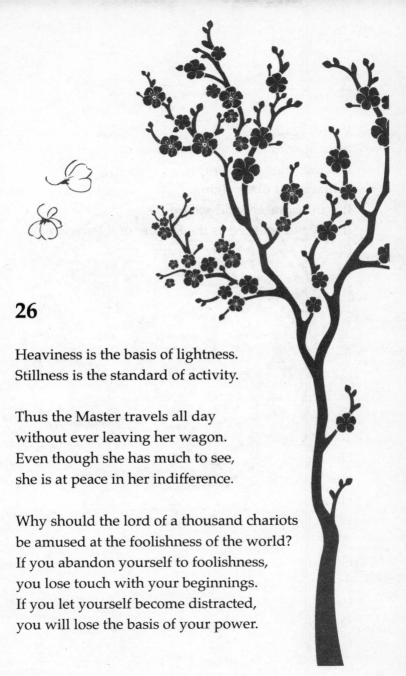

26

Heaviness is the basis of lightness.
Stillness is the standard of activity.

Thus the Master travels all day
without ever leaving her wagon.
Even though she has much to see,
she is at peace in her indifference.

Why should the lord of a thousand chariots
be amused at the foolishness of the world?
If you abandon yourself to foolishness,
you lose touch with your beginnings.
If you let yourself become distracted,
you will lose the basis of your power.

27

A good traveller leaves no tracks,
and a skilful speaker is well rehearsed.
A good bookkeeper has an excellent memory,
and a well-made door is easy to open and needs
    no locks.
A good knot needs no rope and it can not come
    undone.

Thus the Master is willing to help everyone,
and doesn't know the meaning of rejection.
She is there to help all of creation,
and doesn't abandon even the smallest creature.
This is called embracing the light.

What is a good person but a bad person's teacher?
What is a bad person but raw material for his
    teacher?
If you fail to honour your teacher or fail to enjoy
    your student,
you will become deluded no matter how smart
    you are.
It is the secret of prime importance.

28

Know the masculine,
but keep to the feminine:
and become a watershed to the world.
If you embrace the world,
the Tao will never leave you
and you become as a little child.

Know the white,
yet keep to the black:
be a model for the world.
If you are a model for the world,
the Tao inside you will strengthen
and you will return whole to your
      eternal beginning.

Know the honourable,
but do not shun the disgraced:
embracing the world as it is.
If you embrace the world with compassion,
then your virtue will return you to the
Uncarved Block.

The block of wood is carved into utensils
by carving void into the wood.
The Master uses the utensils, yet prefers to keep
    to the block
because of its limitless possibilities.
Great works do not involve discarding substance.

29

Do you want to rule the world and control it?
I don't think it can ever be done.

The world is a sacred vessel
and it can not be controlled.
You will only make it worse if you try.
It may slip through your fingers and disappear.

Some are meant to lead,
and others are meant to follow;
Some must always strain,
and others have an easy time;
Some are naturally big and strong,
and others will always be small;
Some will be protected and nurtured,
and others will meet with destruction.

The Master accepts things as they are,
and out of compassion avoids extravagance,
excess and the extremes.

30

Those who lead people by following the Tao
don't use weapons to enforce their will.
Using force always leads to unseen troubles.

In the places where armies march,
thorns and briars bloom and grow.
After armies take to war,
bad years must always follow.
The skilful commander
strikes a decisive blow, then stops.
When victory is won over the enemy through war
it is not a thing of great pride.
When the battle is over,
arrogance is the new enemy.
War can result when no other alternative is given,
so the one who overcomes an enemy should not
    dominate them.
The strong are always weakened with time.

This is not the way of the Tao.
That which is not of the Tao will soon end.

31

Weapons are the bearers of bad news;
all people should detest them.

The wise man values the left side,
and in time of war he values the right.
Weapons are meant for destruction,
and thus are avoided by the wise.
Only as a last resort
will a wise person use a deadly weapon.
If peace is her true objective
how can she rejoice in the victory of war?
Those who rejoice in victory
delight in the slaughter of humanity.
Those who resort to violence
will never bring peace to the world.
The left side is a place of honour on happy
        occasions.
The right side is reserved for mourning at a funeral.
When the lieutenants take the left side to prepare
        for war,
the general should be on the right side,
because he knows the outcome will be death.
The death of many should be greeted with great
        sorrow,
and the victory celebration should honour those
        who have died.

32

The Tao is nameless and unchanging.
Although it appears insignificant,
nothing in the world can contain it.

If a ruler abides by its principles,
then her people will willingly follow.
Heaven would then reign on earth,
like sweet rain falling on paradise.
People would have no need for laws,
because the law would be written on their hearts.

Naming is a necessity for order,
but naming can not order all things.
Naming often makes things impersonal,
so we should know when naming should end.
Knowing when to stop naming,
you can avoid the pitfall it brings.

All things end in the Tao
just as the small streams and the largest rivers
flow through valleys to the sea.

33

Those who know others are intelligent;
those who know themselves are truly wise.
Those who master others are strong;
those who master themselves have true power.

Those who know they have enough are
    truly wealthy.

Those who persist will reach their goal.

Those who keep their course have a strong will.
Those who embrace death will not perish,
but have life everlasting.

34

The great Tao flows unobstructed in every
    direction.
All things rely on it to conceive and be born,
and it does not deny even the smallest of creation.
When it has accomplished great wonders,
it does not claim them for itself.
It nourishes infinite worlds,
yet it doesn't seek to master the smallest creature.
Since it is without wants and desires,
it can be considered humble.
All of creation seeks it for refuge
yet it does not seek to master or control.
Because it does not seek greatness,
it is able to accomplish truly great things.

35

She who follows the way of the Tao
will draw the world to her steps.
She can go without fear of being injured,
because she has found peace and tranquillity in
    her heart.

Where there is music and good food,
people will stop to enjoy it.
But words spoken of the Tao
seem to them boring and stale.
When looked at, there is nothing for them to see.
When listened for, there is nothing for them
    to hear.
Yet if they put it to use, it would never be
    exhausted.

36

If you want something to return to the source,
you must first allow it to spread out.
If you want something to weaken,
you must first allow it to become strong.
If you want something to be removed,
you must first allow it to flourish.
If you want to possess something,
you must first give it away.

This is called the subtle understanding
of how things are meant to be.

The soft and pliable overcomes the hard and
      inflexible.

Just as fish remain hidden in deep waters,
it is best to keep weapons out of sight.

37

The Tao never acts with force,
yet there is nothing that it cannot do.

If rulers could follow the way of the Tao,
then all of creation would willingly follow their
    example.
If selfish desires were to arise after their
    transformation,
I would erase them with the power of the
    Uncarved Block.

By the power of the Uncarved Block,
future generations would lose their selfish desires.
By losing their selfish desires,
the world would naturally settle into peace.

38

The highest good is not to seek to do good,
but to allow yourself to become it.
The ordinary person seeks to do good things,
and finds that they can not do them continually.

The Master does not force virtue on others,
thus she is able to accomplish her task.
The ordinary person who uses force,
will find that they accomplish nothing.

The kind person acts from the heart,
and accomplishes a multitude of things.
The righteous person acts out of pity,
yet leaves many things undone.
The moral person will act out of duty,
and when no one responds
will roll up his sleeves and use force.

When the Tao is forgotten, there is righteousness.
When righteousness is forgotten, there is morality.
When morality is forgotten, there is the law.
The law is the husk of faith,
and trust is the beginning of chaos.

Our basic understandings are not from the Tao
because they come from the depths of our
    misunderstanding.
The master abides in the fruit and not in the husk.
She dwells in the Tao,
and not with the things that hide it.
This is how she increases in wisdom.

39

The masters of old attained unity with the Tao.
Heaven attained unity and became pure.
The earth attained unity and found peace.
The spirits attained unity so they could minister.
The valleys attained unity that they might be full.
Humanity attained unity that they might flourish.
Their leaders attained unity that they might set
    the example.
This is the power of unity.

Without unity, the sky becomes filthy.
Without unity, the earth becomes unstable.
Without unity, the spirits become unresponsive
and disappear.
Without unity, the valleys become dry as a desert.
Without unity, humankind can't reproduce and
becomes extinct.
Without unity, our leaders become corrupt
and fall.

The great view the small as their source,
and the high take the low as their foundation.
Their greatest asset becomes their humility.
They speak of themselves as orphans and widows,
thus they truly seek humility.
Do not shine like the precious gem,
but be as dull as a common stone.

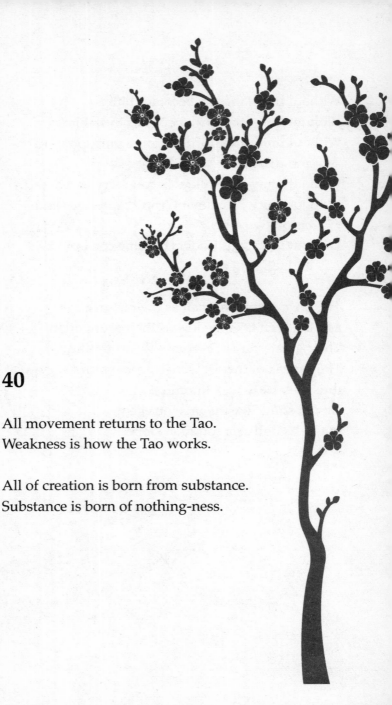

40

All movement returns to the Tao.
Weakness is how the Tao works.

All of creation is born from substance.
Substance is born of nothing-ness.

41

When a superior person hears of the Tao,
she diligently puts it into practice.
When an average person hears of the Tao,
he believes half of it, and doubts the other half.
When a foolish person hears of the Tao,
he laughs out loud at the very idea.
If he didn't laugh,
it wouldn't be the Tao.

Thus it is said:
The brightness of the Tao seems like darkness,
the advancement of the Tao seems like retreat,
the level path seems rough,
the superior path seems empty,
the pure seems to be tarnished,
and true virtue doesn't seem to be enough.
The virtue of caution seems like cowardice,
the pure seems to be polluted,
the true square seems to have no corners,
the best vessels take the most time to finish,
the greatest sounds cannot be heard,
and the greatest image has no form.

The Tao hides in the unnamed,
Yet it alone nourishes and completes all things.

42

The Tao gave birth to One.
The One gave birth to Two.
The Two gave birth to Three.
The Three gave birth to all of creation.

All things carry Yin
yet embrace Yang.
They blend their life breaths
in order to produce harmony.

People despise being orphaned, widowed and
    poor.
But the noble ones take these as their titles.
In losing, much is gained,
and, in gaining, much is lost.

What others teach I too will teach:
'The strong and violent will not die a natural
    death.'

43

That which offers no resistance,
overcomes the hardest substances.
That which offers no resistance
can enter where there is no space.

Few in the world can comprehend
the teaching without words,
or understand the value of non-action.

44

Which is more important, your honour or
    your life?
Which is more valuable, your possessions or
    your person?
Which is more destructive, success or failure?

Great love extracts a great cost
and true wealth requires greater loss.

Knowing when you have enough avoids dishonour,
and knowing when to stop will keep you
    from danger
and bring you a long, happy life.

45

The greatest accomplishments seem imperfect,
yet their usefulness is not diminished.
The greatest fullness seems empty,
yet it will be inexhaustible.

The greatest straightness seems crooked.
The most valued skill seems like clumsiness.
The greatest speech seems full of stammers.

Movement overcomes the cold,
and stillness overcomes the heat.
That which is pure and still is the universal ideal.

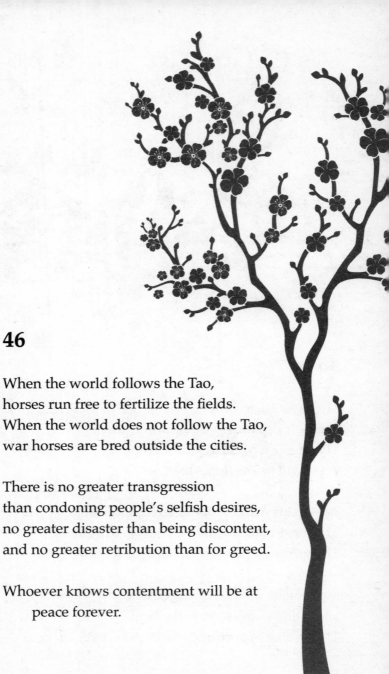

46

When the world follows the Tao,
horses run free to fertilize the fields.
When the world does not follow the Tao,
war horses are bred outside the cities.

There is no greater transgression
than condoning people's selfish desires,
no greater disaster than being discontent,
and no greater retribution than for greed.

Whoever knows contentment will be at
    peace forever.

47

Without opening your door,
you can know the whole world.
Without looking out of your window,
you can understand the way of the Tao.

The more knowledge you seek,
the less you will understand.

The Master understands without leaving,
sees clearly without looking,
accomplishes much without doing anything.

48

One who seeks knowledge learns something
    new every day.
One who seeks the Tao unlearns something
    new every day.
Less and less remains until you arrive at
    non-action.
When you arrive at non-action,
nothing will be left undone.

Mastery of the world is achieved
by letting things take their natural course.
You can not master the world by changing
    the natural way.

49

The Master has no mind of her own.
She understands the mind of the people.

Those who are good she treats as good.
Those who aren't good she also treats as good.
This is how she attains true goodness.

She trusts people who are trustworthy.
She also trusts people who aren't trustworthy.
This is how she gains true trust.

The Master's mind is shut off from the world.
Only for the sake of the people does she muddle
    her mind.
They look to her in anticipation. Yet she treats
    them all as her children.

50

Those who leave the womb at birth
and those who enter their source at death;
of these, three out of ten celebrate life,
three out of ten celebrate death,
and three out of ten simply go from life to death.
What is the reason for this?
Because they are afraid of dying,
therefore they cannot live.

I have heard that those who celebrate life
walk safely among the wild animals.
When they go into battle, they remain unharmed.
The animals find no place to attack them
and the weapons are unable to harm them.
Why? Because they can find no place for death
      in them.

51

The Tao gives birth to all of creation.
The virtue of Tao in nature nurtures them,
and their family gives them their form.
Their environment then shapes them into
    completion.
That is why every creature honours the Tao and
    its virtue.

No one tells them to honour the Tao and
	its virtue,
it happens all by itself.
So the Tao gives them birth,
and its virtue cultivates them,
cares for them,
nurtures them,
gives them a place of refuge and peace,
helps them to grow and shelters them.

It gives them life without wanting to possess
	them,
and cares for them expecting nothing in return.
It is their master, but it does not seek to
	dominate them.
This is called the dark and mysterious virtue.

52

The world had a beginning
which we call the Great Mother.
Once we have found the Mother,
we begin to know what Her children should be.

When we know we are the Mother's child,
we begin to guard the qualities of the Mother in us.
She will protect us from all danger
even if we lose our life.

Keep your mouth closed
and embrace a simple life,
and you will live carefree until the end of
     your days.
If you try to talk your way into a better life,
there will be no end to your trouble.

To understand the small is called clarity.
Knowing how to yield is called strength.
To use your inner light for understanding
regardless of the danger
is called depending on the Constant.

53

If I understood only one thing,
I would want to use it to follow the Tao.
My only fear would be one of pride.
The Tao goes in the level places,
but people prefer to take the short cuts.

If too much time is spent cleaning the house
the land will become neglected and full of weeds,
and the granaries will soon become empty
because there is no one out working the fields.
To wear fancy clothes and ornaments,
to have your fill of food and drink
and to waste all of your money buying possessions
is called the crime of excess.
Oh, how these things go against the way of
        the Tao!

89

54

That which is well built
will never be torn down.
That which is well latched
can not slip away.
Those who do things well
will be honoured from generation to generation.

If this idea is cultivated in the individual,
then his virtue will become genuine.
If this idea is cultivated in your family,
then virtue in your family will be great.
If this idea is cultivated in your community,
then virtue will go a long way.
If this idea is cultivated in your country,
then virtue will be in many places.
If this idea is cultivated in the world,
then virtue will be with everyone.

Then observe the person for what the person does,
and observe the family for what it does,
and observe the community for what it does,
and observe the country for what it does,
and observe the world for what it does.
How do I know this saying is true?
I observe these things and see.

55

One who is filled with the Tao
is like a newborn child.
The infant is protected from
the stinging insects, wild beasts and birds of prey.
Its bones are soft, its muscles are weak,
but its grip is firm and strong.
It doesn't know about the union
of male and female,
yet his penis can stand erect
because of the power of life within him.
It can cry all day and never become hoarse.
This is perfect harmony.

To understand harmony is to understand the
    Constant.
To know the Constant is to be called 'enlightened'.
To unnaturally try to extend life is not appropriate.
To try and alter the life-breath is unnatural.
The master understands that when something
    reaches its prime
it will soon begin to decline.
Changing the natural is against the way of the Tao.
Those who do it will come to an early end.

56

Those who know do not talk.
Those who talk do not know.

Stop talking,
meditate in silence,
blunt your sharpness,
release your worries,
harmonize your inner light,
and become one with the dust.
Doing this is called the dark and mysterious
  identity.

Those who have achieved the mysterious identity
can not be approached, and they can not be
  alienated.
They can not be benefited nor harmed.
They can not be made noble nor to suffer disgrace.
This makes them the most noble of all under the
  heavens.

57

Govern your country with integrity,
weapons of war can be used with great cunning,
but loyalty is only won by not-doing.
How do I know the way things are?
By these:

The more prohibitions you make,
the poorer people will be.
The more weapons you possess,
the greater the chaos in your country.
The more knowledge that is acquired,
the stranger the world will become.
The more laws that you make,
the greater the number of criminals.

Therefore the Master says:
I do nothing,
and people become good by themselves.
I seek peace,
and people take care of their own problems.
I do not meddle in their personal lives,
and the people become prosperous.
I let go of all my desires,
and the people return to the Uncarved Block.

58

If a government is unobtrusive,
the people become whole.
If a government is repressive,
the people become treacherous.

Good fortune has its roots in disaster,
and disaster lurks with good fortune.
Who knows why these things happen,
or when this cycle will end?
Good things seem to change into bad,
and bad things often turn out for good.
These things have always been hard
    to comprehend.

Thus the Master makes things change
without interfering.
She is probing yet causes no harm.
Straightforward, yet does not impose her will.
Radiant, and easy on the eye.

59

There is nothing better than moderation
for teaching people or serving Heaven.
Those who use moderation
are already on the path to the Tao.

Those who follow the Tao early
will have an abundance of virtue.
When there is an abundance of virtue,
there is nothing that cannot be done.
Where there is limitless ability,
then the kingdom is within your grasp.
When you know the Mother of the kingdom,
then you will be long enduring.

This is spoken of as the deep root and the firm
    trunk,
the Way to a long life and great spiritual vision.

60

Governing a large country
is like frying small fish.
Too much poking spoils the meat.

When the Tao is used to govern the world
then evil will lose its power to harm the people.
Not that evil will no longer exist,
but only because it has lost its power.
Just as evil can lose its ability to harm,
the Master shuns the use of violence.

If you give evil nothing to oppose,
then virtue will return by itself.

61

A large country should take the low place like a
     great watershed,
which from its low position assumes the female
     role.
The female overcomes the male by the power of
     her position.
Her tranquillity gives rise to her humility.

If a large country takes the low position,
it will be able to influence smaller countries.
If smaller countries take the lower position,
then they can allow themselves to be influenced.
So both seek to take the lower position
in order to influence the other, or be influenced.

Large countries should desire to protect and help
     the people,
and small countries should desire to serve others.
Both large and small countries benefit greatly
     from humility.

62

The Tao is the tabernacle of creation,
it is a treasure for those who are good,
and a place of refuge for those who are not.

How can those who are not good be abandoned?
Words that are beautiful are worth much,
but good behaviour can only be learned by
     example.

When a new leader takes office,
don't give him gifts and offerings.
These things are not as valuable
as teaching him about the Tao.

Why was the Tao esteemed by the ancient
     Masters?
Is it not said: 'With it we find without looking.
With it we find forgiveness for our transgressions'?
That is why the world cannot understand it.

63

Act by not acting;
do by not doing.
Enjoy the plain and simple.
Find that greatness in the small.
Take care of difficult problems
while they are still easy;
Do easy things before they become too hard.

Difficult problems are best solved while they are
    easy.
Great projects are best started while they are small.
The Master never takes on more than she can
    handle,
which means that she leaves nothing undone.

When an affirmation is given too lightly,
keep your eyes open for trouble ahead.
When something seems too easy,
difficulty is hiding in the details.
The Master expects great difficulty,
so the task is always easier than planned.

64

Things are easier to control while they are quiet.
Things are easier to plan far in advance.
Things break easier while they are still brittle.
Things are easier hid while they are still small.

Prevent problems before they arise.
Take action before things get out of hand.
The tallest tree
begins as a tiny sprout.
The tallest building
starts with one shovel of dirt.
A journey of a thousand miles
starts with a single footstep.

If you rush into action, you will fail.
If you hold on too tight, you will lose your grip.

Therefore the Master lets things take their course
and thus never fails.
She doesn't hold on to things
and never loses them.
By pursuing your goals too relentlessly,
you let them slip away.

If you are as concerned about the outcome
as you are about the beginning,
then it is hard to do things wrong.
The Master seeks no possessions.
She learns by unlearning,
thus she is able to understand all things.
This gives her the ability to help all of creation.

65

The ancient Masters
who understood the way of the Tao,
did not educate people, but made them forget.

Smart people are difficult to guide,
because they think they are too clever.
To use cleverness to rule a country,
is to lead the country to ruin.
To avoid cleverness in ruling a country,
is to lead the country to prosperity.

Knowing the two alternatives is a pattern.
Remaining aware of the pattern is a virtue.
This dark and mysterious virtue is profound.
It is opposite our natural inclination,
but leads to harmony with the heavens.

66

Rivers and seas are rulers
of the streams of hundreds of valleys
because of the power of their low position.

If you want to be the ruler of people,
you must speak to them like you are their servant.
If you want to lead other people,
you must put their interests ahead of your own.

The people will not feel burdened,
if a wise person is in a position of power.
The people will not feel like they are being
        manipulated,
if a wise person is in front as their leader.
The whole world will ask for her guidance,
and will never get tired of her.
Because she does not like to compete,
no one can compete with the things she
        accomplishes.

67

The world talks about honouring the Tao,
but you can't tell it from their actions.
Because it is thought of as great,
the world makes light of it.
It seems too easy for anyone to use.

There are three jewels that I cherish:
compassion, moderation, and humility.
With compassion, you will be able to be brave,
With moderation, you will be able to give to others,
With humility, you will be able to become a great
    leader.
To abandon compassion while seeking to be brave,
or abandoning moderation while being benevolent,
or abandoning humility while seeking to lead
will only lead to greater trouble.
The compassionate warrior will be the winner,
and if compassion is your defence you will be
    secure.
Compassion is the protector of Heaven's salvation.

68

The best warriors
do not use violence.
The best generals
do not destroy indiscriminately.
The best tacticians
try to avoid confrontation.
The best leaders
become servants of their people.

This is called the virtue of non-competition.
This is called the power to manage others.
This is called attaining harmony with the heavens.

69

There is an old saying:
'It is better to become passive
in order to see what will happen.
It is better to retreat a foot
than to advance only an inch.'

This is called
being flexible while advancing,
pushing back without using force,
and destroying the enemy without engaging him.

There is no greater disaster
than underestimating your enemy.
Underestimating your enemy
means losing your greatest assets.
When equal forces meet in battle,
victory will go to the one
that enters with the greatest sorrow.

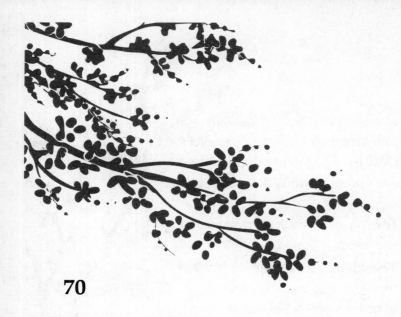

70

My words are easy to understand
and easier to put into practice.
Yet no one in the world seems to understand
    them,
nor are they able to apply what I teach.

My teachings come from the ancients,
the things I do are done for a reason.

Because you do not know me,
you are not able to understand my teachings.
Because those who know me are few,
my teachings become even more precious.

71

Knowing you don't know is wholeness.
Thinking you know is a disease.
Only by recognizing that you have an illness
can you move to seek a cure.

The Master is whole because
she sees her illnesses and treats them,
and thus is able to remain whole.

72

When people become overly bold,
then disaster will soon arrive.

Do not meddle with people's livelihood;
by respecting them they will in turn respect you.

Therefore, the Master knows herself but is not
     arrogant.
She loves herself but also loves others.
This is how she is able to make appropriate
     choices.

73

Being overbold and confident is deadly.
The wise use of caution will keep you alive.

One is the way to death,
and the other is the way to preserve your life.
Who can understand the workings of Heaven?

The Tao of the universe
does not compete, yet wins;
does not speak, yet responds;
does not command, yet is obeyed;
and does not act, but is good at directing.

The nets of Heaven are wide,
but nothing escapes its grasp.

74

If you do not fear death,
then how can it intimidate you?
If you aren't afraid of dying,
there is nothing you cannot do.

Those who harm others
are like inexperienced boys
trying to take the place
of a great lumberjack.
Trying to fill his shoes
will only get them seriously hurt.

75

When people go hungry,
the government's taxes are too high.
When people become rebellious,
the government has become too intrusive.

When people begin to view death lightly,
wealthy people have too much,
which causes others to starve.

Only those who do not cling to their life can
    save it.

76

The living are soft and yielding;
the dead are rigid and stiff.
Living plants are flexible and tender;
the dead are brittle and dry.

Those who are stiff and rigid
are the disciples of death.
Those who are soft and yielding
are the disciples of life.

The rigid and stiff will be broken.
The soft and yielding will overcome.

77

The Tao of Heaven works in the world
like the drawing of a bow.
The top is bent downward;
the bottom is bent up.
The excess is taken from,
and the deficient is given to.

The Tao works to use the excess,
and gives to that which is depleted.
The way of people is to take from the depleted,
and give to those who already have an excess.

Who is able to give to the needy from their excess?
Only someone who is following the way of
    the Tao.

This is why the Master gives,
expecting nothing in return.
She does not dwell on her past accomplishments,
and does not glory in any praise.

78

Water is the softest and most yielding substance.
Yet nothing is better than water,
for overcoming the hard and rigid,
because nothing can compete with it.

Everyone knows that the soft and yielding
overcomes the rigid and hard,
but few can put this knowledge into practice.

Therefore the Master says:
'Only he who is the lowest servant of the kingdom,
is worthy of becoming its ruler.
He who is willing to tackle the most unpleasant
        tasks,
is the best ruler in the world.'

True sayings seem contradictory.

79

Difficulties remain, even after solving a problem.
How, then, can we consider that as good?

Therefore the Master
does what she knows is right,
and makes no demands of others.
A virtuous person will do the right thing,
and persons with no virtue will take advantage
   of others.

The Tao does not choose sides,
the good person receives from the Tao
because she is on its side.

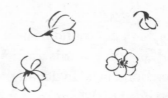

80

Small countries with few people are best.
Give them all of the things they want,
and they will see that they do not need them.
Teach them that death is a serious thing,
and to be content to never leave their homes.
Even though they have plenty
of horses, wagons and boats,
they won't feel that they need to use them.
Even if they have weapons and shields,
they will keep them out of sight.
Let people enjoy the simple technologies,
let them enjoy their food,
let them make their own clothes,
let them be content with their own homes,
and delight in the customs that they cherish.
Although the next country is close enough
that they can hear their roosters crowing and dogs
    barking,
they are content never to visit each other
all of the days of their life.

81

True words do not sound beautiful;
beautiful sounding words are not true.
Wise men don't need to debate;
men who need to debate are not wise.

Wise men are not scholars,
and scholars are not wise.
The Master desires no possessions.
Since the things she does are for the people,
she has more than she needs.
The more she gives to others,
the more she has for herself.

The Tao of Heaven nourishes by not forcing.
The Tao of the Wise Person acts by not competing.